D0533221

More Signs of The Times

A further selection of comic signs from 'The Times Diary'

Elm Tree/ Hamish Hamilton

First published in Great Britain 1975
by Elm Tree Books Ltd.
90 Great Russell Street, London WC1
Copyright © 1975 by Times Newspapers Ltd.
Reprinted September 1978

ISBN 0 241 89296 1

Printed photolitho in Great Britain by
Ebenezer Baylis and Son Limited
The Trinity Press, Worcester, and London

FOREWORD

The first collection of road signs from *The Times Diary* was published a year ago, and the intervening 12 months have been a worrying time in most respects. Inflation and unemployment have increased, the pound has wavered and we have been told incessantly that national doom is just around the corner, if not already here.

I am glad, therefore, to be able to report a steady improvement in respect of misleading, ambiguous or otherwise risible road signs. The authorities in Britain and elsewhere have obliged by maintaining a high standard of absurdity, and readers of *The Times* have responded magnificently and in large numbers by photographing them and sending them to me. Thus we are able to produce a second volume of the signs, each one guaranteed different from any in volume one.

Moreover, the series in *The Times Diary* has spawned imitators. The *Sunday Times* flirted with the idea for a time and so did *That's Life*, Esther Rantzen's programme on BBC Television. Yet the supply has been sufficient for all three markets, even if sometimes the other two have seemed to duplicate signs first shown in *The Times*.

No part of any newspaper was immune last year from references to the persistent economic crisis, and a few of our road signs related to it —like 'Upper class exit', photographed at a Kenya railway station, and 'Economy Road—cul-de-sac', which is to be seen in Lowestoft.

As the supply of home-grown signs began to dwindle, readers made up for the lack by sending them from all parts of the globe. East Africa and Sri Lanka seem, for an unknown reason, the most fertile ground. My favourite among these was from Uganda, urging visitors to Entebbe Zoo not to feed the animals. 'If you have any suitable food, please give it to the guard on duty.' From Singapore, I liked the one forbidding overtaking 'for the next 200 years'. And of the many from America, the one we received from San Francisco struck me as a fine example of the notice which conveys alarming information without offering guidance as to what you are supposed to do about it: 'This building does not meet the structural standards imposed by law for earthquake safety.'

From the home market, I think my favourites this year were the surely superfluous 'This staircase ends here', from Jersey, 'Parking allowed only on both sides of this road', and, from Ireland, 'Same day cleaners—48-hour service'.

Given a reasonably sustained rate of inventiveness among our sign writers, and no undue increases in the price of cameras, film or postage, there seems little reason why the series should not continue indefinitely. My thanks are due to all those who have entered into the spirit of the thing by sending photographs, both those we have used and those we have not.

The value people place on getting their signs printed was proved when I inadvertently attributed one to the wrong man. The real photographer—a military man—rang angrily, pointing out that the man to whom we had wrongly attributed it—another soldier—was coincidentally known to him and he could not possibly have taken the picture as he had never been near the place in question.

People who have failed to get their photographs published can console themselves with the knowledge that the acceptance rate is only about one in five, and that round the next corner there might be the most hilarious sign ever. So cameras at the ready and keep your eyes on the road.

Michael Leapman
Editor of *The Times Diary*

These contradictory signs sharing a post in Ross-on-Wye were photographed by A. E. Idle.

A quaint but unhelpful road sign in Canton, China, photographed by
Lailan Young of Hackney.

· NOTICE ·

This Building Does Not Meet The Structural Standards imposed by Law for Earth Quake Safety

This sign was snapped in California by Andrew Charles of Halstead.

SLOW
(CONCEALED ENTRANCES)
NO OVERTAKING FOR
THE NEXT 200 YRS

Colonel J. H. Hild of Salisbury photographed this long-term road sign in Singapore.

HEALTH FOOD & KOSHER
FLOWERS

This sign will mystify Jewish readers in particular. Leon Shirlaw of
Romford photographed it in Selfridge's Food Department before it
was converted to a supermarket.

These road signs, the most permissive seen so far, were photographed in La Bourboule, France, by Richard Lawn.

A notable announcement of the obvious, snapped by F. S. Osborn of Hornsey, at the headquarters of the Department of the Environment in Westminster.

This sign was photographed near Dublin, some distance from the Giant's Causeway, by Eric Shephard of Banbury.

Anthony Henfrey photographed this sign in Sicamous, British
Columbia.

A 52
DERBY

A 609
ILKESTON

A 610
RIPLEY

ALTERNATIVE

ROUTE

This bewildering road sign was photographed in Nottingham by Roderick Hole.

An alarming road sign, photographed near Swanage by Eric Smith of Bristol.

OVERCOATS RAINCOATS
CLOTHES AND **CLERGYMEN**

This sign was photographed near St Peter's in Rome by Francis Fitzgibbon of St John's Wood. It shows a shop dealing in a catholic variety of merchandise.

This road sign was photographed in Ludlow by John Godrich who lives there, but who cannot explain the mystery of the buses with depressible roofs.

This sign was photographed on the Windsor relief road by Hans Schmoller, who believes it has been erected for the benefit of visiting Australians.

This pair of road signs was snapped by Mark Rubinstein of Kensington, outside a car park by the leaning tower of Pisa.

A contradictory sign, photographed at Butchart Gardens, British Columbia, by Dr Ian Adamson of Dundee University.

D. G. Bowtell of Burton-on-the-Wolds photographed this baffling pair of road signs in North Yorkshire.

This sign, which takes road courtesy to the extreme, was photographed by A. M. Taylor at Cricket St Thomas, in Somerset.

Peter Ferner of Sale, Cheshire, photographed this piece of cruelty to buses at the intersection of M65 and M56.

This sign, photographed by Heather Holden-Brown near Cape Point, South Africa, shows no great confidence in its own efficacy.

PARTY ROOM
AVAILABLE

HOT MEALS
DELIVERED
OR
TAKEN AWAY

THE
DRAGON
CHINESE
RESTAURANT

This sign, advertising a comprehensive and probably a unique service, was photographed by J. Burgess outside a Chinese restaurant in Norwich.

WARNING
THIS IS NOT BALLACHULISH FERRY

A mysteriously negative sign, photographed in Argyllshire by Libby Weir-Breen of Edinburgh.

This sign, which might qualify for the record book, was photographed on Exmoor by J. C. Rustad of Pulborough.

Glynis Fell, of Cambridge, photographed this politically motivated sign in Nakuru Station, Kenya.

This sign indicates the freight office at Hell, north of Trondheim, Norway. The Reverend George Austin, who sent the picture, reports that when you get there Hell is a very dull place.

An encouraging sign which gives the aspiring climber some uplift in the neighbourhood of the Eiger, where it was photographed by Sydney Bailey of Finchley.

G. Black of Chipping Campden photographed this frank sign on the road from Nowshera to Peshawar in Pakistan.

A monument to the linguistic gap between Britain and North America, this sign was photographed on Vancouver Island, Canada, by Helen Hadfield of Denham.

This understated sign was photographed in Jersey by Jack Sanguinetti of Hindhead, Surrey.

This puzzling sign was photographed at an underpass in the Barbican,
London, by E. Stekel of Harringay, who says that although he
measures less than 15′ 8″, he has no difficulty passing through.

Simon Alsop of Ilford photographed this churlishly unhelpful road
sign in Australia on the toll road between Sydney and Newcastle.

Raise legs before moving

This clear and unchallengeable sign was submitted by two readers. It appears on the back of mobile huts with retractable legs. This snap is by David Howard of Highbury.

庭園へ

園

庭別

館

← —————————

No Loitering

without permission

宿泊以外の方

庭園ご散策ご希望の方は

事務所にお申出下さい

This appealing sign was photographed outside a Japanese inn by
Harold Rose of Highgate, who does not say whether he spotted anyone
requesting permission to loiter.

Photographed in Co. Wicklow by Captain C. Fletcher-Wood of the Royal Artillery, this sign confirms comfortingly that the days are getting longer.

外宾·国际·海员止步
GUESTS & SEAMEN
NO ADMITTANCE

This sign was photographed by L. McCormick-Goodhart, of Virginia, U.S.A. It was taken in China in the grounds of the Shanghai Friendship Store, where friendship seems rather selective.

This biological curiosity was spotted on a road near Winkfield, Berkshire, by W. H. C. Saxon of Hemel Hempstead.

Photographed by Charles Parr, of Oxford, this sign warns of an apparently rare hazard in Cochin, India.

A plaintive sign photographed at Entebbe Zoo, Uganda, in 1963, by Bernard Parry of Leyburn, Yorkshire.

This sign was photographed in York by Peter Gray, who lives there.

J. R. Martin photographed this mystifying sign near his office in Nairobi, Kenya.

FOOT WEARING PROHIBITED

SOCKS NOT ALLOWED

This sign, with its alarming implications, stands at the entrance of a temple in Rangoon. Major Ventham, of Camberley, who took the picture, did not dare investigate further.

DON'T LET WORRY KILL YOU OFF - LET THE CHURCH HELP

John Cordeaux, Manager of BBC Radio Humberside, photographed this sign outside Newland Methodist Church in Hull.

Photographed by Greta Williams of Ipswich, this sign appears in the town only on Saturdays, when traffic is angrier than at other times of the week.

This bewildering sign was photographed by Captain S. Chalmers of Gillingham.

JET BLAST
IS DANGEROUS
Passengers Only
BEYOND THIS POINT

Irene Hunter of Chelsea photographed this example of the doubtful privileges which can be purchased with airline tickets at Austin airport in Texas.

THE DEPARTMENT OF THE ENVIRONMENT

DRIVING TESTS
FIRST FLOOR

This sign, which Dr Tessa Rajak of Primrose Hill photographed in North Yorkshire, may be in the Department of the Environment's bid to keep learner drivers out of road accidents.

PECIAL FORCE TRAINING AREA
RESTRICTED TO UNAUTHORISED
PERSONS

an Linn of Exeter University photographed this bewildering sign
etween Masindi and Butiaba in Uganda.

MORETON CORBET CASTLE

ADMISSION

	WEEKDAYS	SUNDAYS
MAR - APR	9·30 - 5·30	2 - 5·30
MAY - SEPT	9·30 - 7	2 - 7
OCTOBER	9·30 - 5·30	2 - 5·30
NOV - FEB	9·30 - 4	2 - 4

ADULTS   FREE EACH

CHILDREN (UNDER 15)   EACH

SPECIAL RATES FOR PARTIES

THIS MONUMENT IS IN THE CARE OF THE MINISTRY OF WORKS IT IS AN OFFENCE TO INJURE OR DEFACE IT

I. D. Wilson of Admaston, Shropshire, photographed this mystifying sign at Morton Corbet Castle.

THIS ENTRANCE IS IN USE BY CONTRACTORS CHILDREN AND THE PUBLIC ARE WARNED NOT TO USE IT

This sign, denoting the effects of an upbringing among heavy building equipment, was spotted by Neil MacFadyen on the main gate of Greenwich pier.

This magical pair of signs was photographed at La Roche-en-Ardenne, Belgium, by A. P. Holwell of Sunderland.

Irene Bee of Lancaster photographed this sign near the Pilgrim Monument at Plymouth, Massachusetts, where they clearly expect a high rate of absent-mindedness among visitors.

Miss J. B. Clark of Chelsea photographed this pair of signs on the Isle of Harris.

James Leach of Bromley photographed this sign in North London.

An anticipation of the ultimate deterrent for private patients, this sign was photographed by R. S. Illingworth of Sheffield.